A Taste of Culture

Foods of Brazil

Barbara Sheen

KIDHAVEN PRESS
A part of Gale, Cengage Learning

GALE
CENGAGE Learning

Detroit • New York • San Francisco • New Haven, Conn • Waterville, Maine • London

© 2008 Gale, Cengage Learning

For more information, contact
KidHaven Press
27500 Drake Rd.
Farmington Hills, MI 48331-3535
Or you can visit our Internet site at gale.cengage.com

LIBRARY OF CONGRESS CATALOGING-IN-PUBLICATION DATA
Barbara Sheen.
Foods of Brazil / by Barbara Sheen.
p. cm. — (A taste of culture)
Includes bibliographical references and index.
ISBN 978-0-7377-3773-8 (hardcover)
1. Cookery, Brazilian—Juvenile literature. I. Title.
TX716.B6S49 2007
641.5981—dc22
2007021859

ISBN-10: 0-7377-3773-5

Printed in the United States of America
3 4 5 6 7 12 11 10 09 08

Contents

Food Rooted in the Past

Brazil is a large country blessed with a fine climate and fertile soil. These conditions make food plentiful. Dozens of varieties of tropical fruit and nuts grow wild in the rain forest here. The coastal waters of the Atlantic Ocean and the inland waters of the Amazon River are full of water creatures. Herds of cattle thrive on the Brazilian plains or **pampas** (pahm-pahs). Corn and other vegetables grow well on Brazilian farms.

Brazilian cooks have many foods to choose from. They use them all in their cooking. But it is **manioc** (mah-nee-oc), beans, and rice that Brazilian cooks depend on. These are the same staples that the ancestors of modern Brazilians, the Amerindians, the Portuguese, and the West Africans could not do without. Brazilian meals would be incomplete without them.

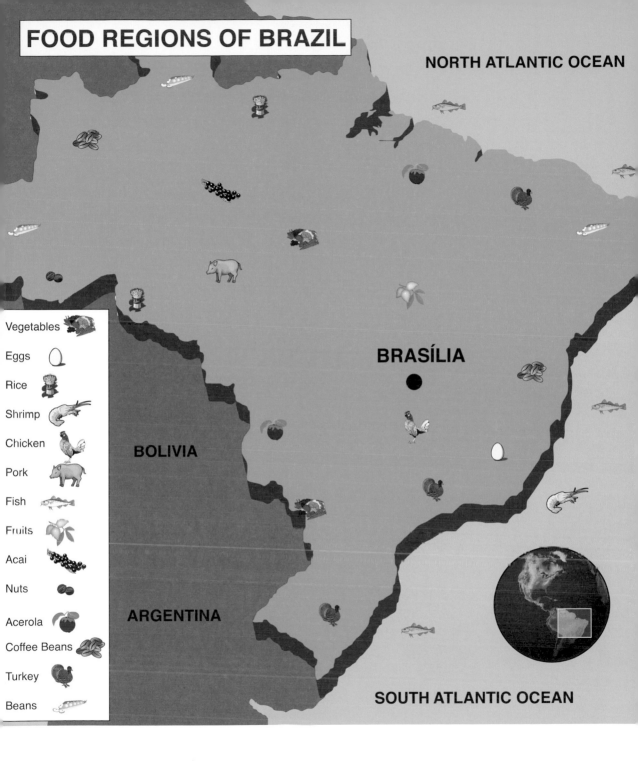

FOOD REGIONS OF BRAZIL

NORTH ATLANTIC OCEAN

BRASÍLIA

BOLIVIA

ARGENTINA

SOUTH ATLANTIC OCEAN

Vegetables

Eggs

Rice

Shrimp

Chicken

Pork

Fish

Fruits

Acai

Nuts

Acerola

Coffee Beans

Turkey

Beans

A Starchy Root

Brazilians have been eating manioc, which is also known as cassava, yuca (u-ca), or mandioca (mahn-dee-oh-cah), for hundreds of years. This starchy root vegetable was a staple food of the Tupi (Too-pee) Indians, a native tribe that lived along the Amazon River.

Manioc looks like a large sweet potato. It is long and thin and covered by tough brown skin. Inside, it contains snow-white flesh. It also contains a poisonous juice that must be removed before the vegetable can be eaten. The Tupi Indians used a tube made of woven plant fibers to squeeze the juice out of the vegetable. Then they boiled the manioc, eating

Brazilians have been eating manioc for centuries.

Farofa, toasted manioc, is used as a condiment in many Brazilian dishes.

it like boiled potatoes. Or they ground it into nutty tasting flour called **farinha de mandioca** (fah-rin-ah day mahn-dee-oh-cah). They mixed the flour with ground fish. And they toasted it in the sun to make **farofa** (fahr-oh-fah). It is a substance similar to fine bread crumbs. The Indians ate it like porridge, as well as used it as a seasoning.

Modern Brazilians still eat farofa. In fact, it is the most popular condiment in Brazil. Just as salt and pepper are found on most North American tables, a saucer of farofa is found on every Brazilian table. Brazilians sprinkle it over meat, fish, rice, beans, and vegetables. It adds a toasted nutty flavor that Brazilians have adored for centuries. "No Brazilian table," says chef Christopher Idone, "is without it."[1]

Interesting Fish

The Amazon River runs through Brazil. It contains more water than any other river in the world. It also contains many interesting fish.

Pirarucu (pee-rah-rue-cue) is one of the most interesting. It is the largest freshwater fish in the world. It can weigh more than 400 pounds (181kg) and measure up to 15 feet (4m) long. Brazilians eat pirarucu, which tastes something like chicken, in coconut sauce. And they turn the fish's tough scales into fingernail files.

Giant piranhas are another popular Amazon River fish that Brazilians like to eat. These ferocious fish not only eat other fish, they eat land animals that wander into the river. Their teeth are so sharp that Brazilian fishermen must be careful when handling them.

Pirarucu is the largest freshwater fish in the world.

Farofa is not the only way Brazilians use manioc. They use manioc flour to make cuscus (coos-coos), a sweet breakfast pudding that is sold door-to-door in many Brazilian villages. Other sweets are made from tapioca, a special type of flour made from manioc.

Fried manioc is another Brazilian favorite. The vegetable is sliced and cooked like French fries. But the taste, according to many Brazilians, is starchier and more satisfying. Maria, a Web-based Brazilian cookbook author explains, "many people I know say that fried manioc beats potatoes anytime."[2]

Beans

Beans were another important part of the Indians' diet. In 1500, the Portuguese explorer Pedro Álvars Cabral claimed Brazil for Portugal. Thirty years later, Portuguese settlers started arriving. They adopted many of the foods the Indians ate, including beans, which soon became an essential part of their diet.

The West Africans that the Portuguese brought to Brazil to work as slaves on Brazilian sugar plantations also loved beans. Besides eating the beans that were native to Brazil, they brought other varieties, such as black-eyed peas, with them. They added spicy chile peppers, coconut milk, and dried shrimp to the beans to give them new and distinctive Brazilian flavors. Beans were so important to the Africans' diet that they prepared special bean dishes to honor their gods.

Beans are very important to Brazilian cuisine and are eaten at least once every day.

Beans are just as important to modern Brazilians as they were to their ancestors. To Brazilians, a native explains, beans "are like oxygen."[3] In fact, Brazil is the world's largest grower and consumer of beans. White beans, black beans, red beans, and brown beans are all grown and eaten here. Although every type of bean is popular, black beans are among everyone's favorites.

Most Brazilians eat beans at least once, and often twice, a day. Cooks make a big pot of beans at least once a week. The beans cook for hours until they are soft and tender. When they are almost done, the cook takes some of the beans out of the pot, crushes them into a paste, and then puts them back. This thickens the bean sauce giving it a velvety texture. Spices, onions, or pork may be added depending on the cook. Chef

Black Beans

Traditionally, Brazilians make black beans with dried beans that take hours to cook. Using canned black beans is faster and easier.

Ingredients
15-oz. can black beans
½ onion, chopped
1 garlic clove, chopped
3 tablespoons olive oil
7 oz. cooked turkey or pork sausage, sliced into
   small chunks

Instructions
1. Heat the oil in a pot large enough to hold the beans. Add the onions and garlic and lightly fry until the onions are soft and lightly cooked.
2. Add the beans and sausage to the pot. Stir.
3. Cook on medium to low heat until the mixture comes to a boil. Stir to keep the beans from sticking to the pot.

Serves 4.

Michael Bateman explains, "every family has its own way of preparing and flavoring them."[4]

When the beans are done, they are eaten whole as an accompaniment to meat or fish. Leftover beans may be mashed and mixed with farofa. Or the mashed beans are fried, like potatoes. They may be stuffed into pastries, formed into fritters, or added to soups and stews. Black bean soup topped with sliced egg, for example, is a Brazilian favorite. So is a rich pork and bean stew. No matter how they are used, one thing is certain, when the beans are all gone, there is bound to be a fresh pot on the stove.

Rice

Beans are almost always served with rice, another important staple food in Brazil. A bowl of rice and a bowl of beans are standard accompaniments for fish, seafood, meat, and poultry. And when rice and beans are combined, they are a meal in themselves.

Rice is not native to Brazil. The Portuguese brought the grain with them. It grew well in Brazil's rich soil and soon became an important part of the Brazilian diet. Brazilian chef Dolores Botafogo explains, "everyone eats rice in Brazil, from the richest to the poorest, and when you have tried some of our typical rice dishes, you will see why."[5]

Not just any rice will do. Brazilians are particular about their rice. They like it long grain and fluffy, with every grain separate. Perfect rice takes careful

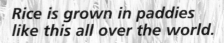

Rice is grown in paddies like this all over the world.

Brazilian Rice

This recipe uses traditional rice. Instant rice can be substituted. If instant rice is used, follow the cooking time on the package.

Ingredients
2 cups long-grain white rice
4 cups water
1 teaspoon salt
½ onion, chopped
4-oz. can diced tomatoes with liquid
1 garlic clove, chopped
2 tablespoons olive oil

Instructions
1. Heat the oil over medium heat. Add the onions, garlic, and tomatoes with liquid, and cook until the onions are lightly browned, stirring often.
2. Add the rice. Stir so that the rice is covered with oil.
3. Add the water and bring the mixture to a boil on medium heat. When the mixture boils, reduce the heat to low, cover the pot, and let the rice cook until all the liquid is absorbed and the rice is tender, about 20 minutes. Turn off the heat but leave the rice in the covered pot for another 5 minutes.
Serves 4.

Long-grain rice is a staple item in the Brazilian diet.

Brazilians use rice not only to accompany meals but also to create colorful meat dishes such as this.

preparation. Although many Brazilians simply boil rice, some cooks first lightly fry the rice in oil with garlic, onions, and cilantro, an herb Brazilians love. Brazilians inherited this cooking method, known as **refogado** (ray-foo-gah-doh) from the Portuguese. It adds flavor to the

Food Shopping in Brazil

Brazil has many large modern supermarkets. There are also many outdoor markets where fresh fruits, vegetables, cheeses, eggs, fish, meat, chicken, and flowers are sold. Most of these markets are held on a specific day of the week. Shoppers find rows and rows of tented stalls at these markets. There are usually piles of fresh exotic fruits, baskets of brightly colored chile peppers, fresh greens, ground spices, and dried beans. There may be live chickens and goats. And, depending on the region of Brazil, there may also be parrots and even pet monkeys for sale.

Outdoor markets are colorful and filled with fruits, vegetables, cheeses, meat, and flowers.

rice, which is then boiled in water. Sometimes coconut milk, the liquid that is extracted from mature coconut meat, is added to the rice. It gives the rice a sweet creamy flavor and a fragrant aroma. "Cooking rice properly, so that every grain is separate, well cooked, but not sticky, is an art, and when onions and other seasonings are added, it is good enough to serve at a banquet,"[6] says Botafogo.

Besides serving rice as a tasty accompaniment to meals, Brazilians mix it with meat, fish, poultry, fruit, and vegetables to create delicious main dishes like rice with chicken, sausage, bacon, and tomatoes, or rice with shrimp. Colored rice, rice with carrots, bacon, and raisins, is another favorite. So is rice with fried bananas, ham, and hard-boiled eggs. Rice is also a popular dessert. Rice pudding topped with melted sugar and cinnamon is eaten all over Brazil.

The Brazilian people do love rice, beans, and manioc. Just as their ancestors did, modern Brazilian cooks depend on these same staple ingredients to create delicious dishes that are uniquely Brazilian.

Chapter 2

Different Regions, Different Dishes

Brazil is the fifth-largest country in the world. Mountains, rain forests, plains, rolling hills, and sandy tropical beaches are all part of the Brazilian landscape. Consequently, different products are raised throughout the nation. For instance, cattle are raised on the southern plains. Seafood and fish dominate on the coasts and along the Amazon River, while fruits and nuts grow wild in the tropical rain forests of the north. This diversity has led each region to develop its own favorite dishes. Although these dishes have their origins in a particular region, they have become favorites throughout the nation.

Hills, beaches, and rain forest are only part of Brazil's diverse landscape.

The National Dish

Feijoada (fay-jwa-dah) is the national dish of Brazil, and it has been for more than 300 years. This rich bean-and-pork stew originated in the southeastern part of the country. African slaves working on sugar plantations near Rio de Janeiro created it.

For their food, the slaves were given only the poorest cuts of meat, such as pig's feet, ears, tails, and knuckles. To make the otherwise tough meat tasty, they cooked it slowly for as long as a day with black beans and spices. This ensured that the flavors mixed well and the meat became tender. Although the stew was originally considered food for slaves, the delicious aroma coming from the cooking pot soon tempted the plantation owners to try it. Before long, it became a favorite with everyone. "This dish became traditional all over the country," explains an article on Brazilmax. com, a Web site dedicated to Brazilian culture. It is "a famous entrée that everybody who visits Brazil has to taste."[7]

Today, better cuts of meat are used. Depending on the cook, because every Brazilian cook has his or her own special recipe, as many as a dozen different cuts of meat are likely to find their way into the stew pot. These include pork loin, bacon, sausage, tongue, salted pork, and spare ribs. The meat is slowly simmered with black beans, garlic, onions, chile peppers. When it is done, the stew is thick, incredibly fragrant, and almost black in color.

Feijoada, a bean-and-pork stew, is the national dish of Brazil.

Because it takes so long to prepare, feijoada is a Saturday tradition.

A Saturday Tradition

Because it takes hours to prepare, feijoada is typically eaten on Saturdays. This gives cooks plenty of time to prepare it and diners plenty of time to enjoy the rich dish, which is served with many accompaniments. "The meal," Brazilian food and travel expert Joan Peterson says, "takes many hours to prepare and almost as much time to eat. . . . Much of the day is devoted to partaking of this dish."[8]

The meat and beans are served on separate platters. Often, the tongue is placed in the middle of the meat platter and the other meats are placed around it. Diners select the meats they prefer. Rice, finely shredded

Kale Brazil Style

Brazilians eat kale as an accompaniment to feijoada. It is easy to make and has a crispy texture. If kale is not available, collard greens can be used.

Ingredients
1 pound kale
½ onion, chopped
1 garlic clove, chopped
2 tablespoons olive oil
salt and pepper to taste

Instructions
1. Cut off the stems of the kale. Wash and drain the kale.
2. Roll each leaf into a cylinder and cut the kale crosswise into thin strips.
3. Heat the oil in a frying pan over medium heat. Add the onions and garlic. Fry until they are lightly browned.
4. Add the kale. Stir-fry for 4–5 minutes. Do not overcook the kale. It should keep its bright green color.
5. Add salt and pepper to taste.

Serves 4.

Green, leafy kale is often served with feijoada.

stir-fried kale, hot sauce, orange slices, and farofa accompany the stew. The meal, according to chef Norman Van Aken, "is a treasured part of the Brazilian table."[9]

A Cowboy Feast

Most Brazilians love beef and eat it often. As a matter of fact, Brazilians were the first people in South America to raise cattle, which they started doing more than 400 years ago. Brazilian cowboys, or **gauchos** (gow-chohs) as they are known in Brazil, developed a way of cooking beef that was perfectly suited to their wandering life. The dish they created is called **churrasco** (chur-rahs-coh). It is a favorite dish throughout the nation.

In the past, hungry gauchos killed and butchered a steer right out on the pampas. Then, the gaucho hung the meat on the end of an iron spit. He stuck the spit into the ground on an angle that let the meat hang over a pit of burning firewood. While the meat slowly cooked, the

Churrasco, barbecued meat Brazilian style, is a favorite meal.

Gauchos, or Brazilian cowboys, have been raising cattle for hundreds of years.

gaucho used an iron teapot to baste it with salt water. The salt tenderized the meat, and the water kept it from burning. Once the meat was brown, the gaucho cut off bite-sized pieces with his knife. He sprinkled it with farofa and used his knife to transfer the hot juicy meat to his mouth.

Today, diners use both a knife and a fork to eat churrasco. And the barbequed meat usually includes a variety of meats such as steaks, sausages, pork, and chicken. The meats are usually served with a number of different salads, fried onion rings, a sauce made of onions, vinegar, and chile peppers, and of course, farofa.

Brazilians eat churrasco at special restaurants that specialize in the dish. And they make it in their own backyards. Just as many North Americans have backyard grills, many Brazilians have their own built-in churrasco pits lined with bricks. "We like to invite

Weighing In

Brazilians like to eat out and have many different types of restaurants. One of the most interesting is a per kilo restaurant. Here, diners pile whatever food items they want on a plate. The food is then weighed to determine the price. So, someone who loves rice can select lots of rice and less meat. Or, a vegetable lover can get a heaping mound of vegetables. This makes eating at a per kilo restaurant economical. Diners do not pay for more food than they can eat. It also ensures that people with large appetites get enough to eat.

Moqueca

Brazilians use dende oil to make moqueca. Olive or peanut oil is a good substitute. Firm white fish or chicken tenders can be used instead of shrimp.

Ingredients
2 tablespoons olive oil
1 small onion, chopped
2 garlic cloves, chopped
juice of 1 large lime
4-oz. can chopped green chiles, drained
$2/3$ cup coconut milk
20 shrimp, cleaned and shelled
1 bunch fresh cilantro, chopped
2 tomatoes, chopped

Instructions
1. Put the shrimp in a bowl with the lime juice. Refrigerate for at least 15 minutes.
2. Heat the oil in a pan over medium heat. Add the onions, garlic, and chiles. Stir-fry for 3 minutes.
3. Add all the remaining ingredients. Cook over medium heat until the shrimp are cooked, about 5 minutes.
4. Serve with rice.

Serves 4.

Moqueca is a seafood stew originally brought to Brazil by African slaves.

groups of friends to eat churrasco in our own backyards or at our country homes or farms,"[10] explains Botafogo.

But no matter where churrasco is served, everyone is in for a treat when they bite into this fall-apart tender meat with its smoky scent and flavor.

A Delicious Stew

Moqueca (moh-keh-cah) is a delicious seafood stew that comes from northeastern Brazil. It takes advantage of the fresh fish, seafood, and tropical plants so plentiful in that region. Former African slaves in the Brazilian state of Bahia developed moqueca. It is quite similar to fish stews popular in West Africa. It combines seafood with vegetables, coconut milk, hot chile peppers, and **dende** (den-day) **oil**. The last is red-orange oil that comes from an African palm tree. The slaves brought the palm seeds with them.

The use of dende oil, which is thicker and richer tasting than other vegetable oils, characterizes the food of this part of Brazil. It is so popular here that its fragrance fills the air. It, says food writer and frequent visitor to Bahia, Manny Howard, "gives off a nutty aroma that permeates everything—our clothes, our hair, even the patio outside the . . . kitchen."[11]

To make moqueca, cooks lightly fry their choice of seafood in the brightly colored oil, along with onions, tomatoes, cilantro, lime juice, chile peppers, and coconut milk. Instead of using a traditional metal frying pan, many cooks opt for the same kind of handmade clay pan that Brazilians have been cooking in for more

Foods from the Rain Forest

The Amazon rain forest is the largest rain forest in the world. Almost one-third the size of the United States, it is home to about half of the world's living things, including many popular foods. These include dozens of different fruits, such as bananas and citrus fruits. Nuts like cashews, Brazil nuts, and cola nuts used to make soda also grow here. So do beans, peppers, okra, vanilla, coffee beans, tea, and chocolate.

The rain forest is also home to hundreds of different herbs and medicinal plants. In fact, 37 percent of all the medicines used in the United States are derived from Amazon rain forest plants.

Many different kinds of nuts grow in the Amazon rain forest.

than 400 years. They say that the clay keeps the seafood moist and the stew from drying out.

No matter the pan, only the freshest seafood is used. Typically, the ingredients for moqueca go from the sea to the cooking pan in a matter of hours. Mussels, clams, crab, or fish are all top choices. But shrimp is probably the most popular seafood for moqueca. Cooks do not remove the heads or the

Plantains, which look like green bananas, accompany many Brazilian meals.

shells. Brazilians eat them whole. The head, they insist, is the sweetest part.

The stew is cooked for about an hour. As it cooks, the moqueca picks up the bright orange-red hue of the oil. Once the sauce has thickened, it is ready. It is often served with rice and accompanied by fried manioc or plantains, which look like green bananas. Other vegetables and hot sauce are served too. The resulting dish smells of the oil, the coconuts, and the sea. It tastes slightly sweet and spicy. It is, according to Rosa, a cook with her own blog, "a concentration of what Brazil has to offer: beautiful sweet flavors tinted by the exotic."[12]

Moqueca, feijoada, and churrasco are all a blend of delicious ingredients and flavors that represent the different regions of Brazil where they originated. With their tempting tastes and aromas, it is no wonder they are favorite dishes throughout Brazil.

Tasty Snacks and Healthy Drinks

Brazilians love to snack. **Salgadihos** (sal-gah-dee-yohs), which means little salty treats, are sold everywhere—on street corners, in small shops, on roadsides, at beaches, and at public events. Vendors tempt hungry Brazilians with a wide range of delicious choices. And, when Brazilians get thirsty, juice bars offer freshly squeezed juices in dozens of exotic flavors.

Tiny Pies

Salgadihos are sold all over Brazil. Most are baked or fried pastries made with meat, beans, cheese, vegetables, fish, or seafood. **Empadinhas**, (em-pah-deen-yahs) are among everyone's favorite. These are tiny pies that are baked until their crusts are soft and

30

Tiny pies, called empadinhas, are a favorite snack.

Although Brazil has many modern supermarkets, much food is still sold at outdoor stands.

flaky. Inside, they contain a delectable surprise. They are packed with just about anything—potatoes, spicy ground chicken, cheese, ham, vegetables, and, above all, shrimp. Not just shrimp alone, but shrimp mixed with tomatoes, onions, peppers, cilantro, and olives. In fact, every filling features a mix of flavors and spices that makes the little pies irresistible. Brazilian author Maria says, "empadinhas are totally yummy tiny pies . . . One of the first things I do when I arrive in Rio is go to my favorite doceira [snack shop] . . . and snack on these delicious Brazilian creations. I love them all."[13]

Fried Favorites

When an empadinha is fried, rather than baked, it is called a **pastel** (pass-tel). Pastels are just one of the many fried salgadihos that Brazilians enjoy. **Acarajes** (ah-cah-rah-es) are another. They are zesty bean fritters that originated in Africa. What makes them uniquely Brazilian is the dried shrimps that are added to the batter. In the past, Brazilians dried shrimp to keep them from spoiling. Today they dry shrimp because they like their crunchy taste.

Just as in the past, shrimp are dried out in the sun. Christopher Idone describes the process: "In the scorching sun, hills of shrimp are tossed and raked over and over again, then at night covered with a tarp. The process is repeated over the next couple of days until the shells are crisp and crunchy and the flesh tender but a little chewy."[14]

For acarajes, the dried shrimp are ground into a powder that is mixed with mashed and skinned brown beans and chile flakes. The batter is fried in dende oil until the little cakes are crisp and golden. Street vendors prepare the spicy treats in big pans right on the street. Usually, the vendors are women dressed in the distinctive costume of Bahia—a turban and a big white skirt. If customers like, the vendor will split the fritter open and pour on one of two sauces. The first is made with shrimp, chile peppers, cilantro, and ginger. The second adds coconut milk and nuts to the mix. With or without sauce, acarajes have a crisp tangy flavor that is yummy.

Shrimp are added to many different Brazilian dishes.

"It's hard to beat a good acaraje,"[15] declares an article on Bahia-Online, a Web site promoting Brazilian travel.

Little Purses

Pamonhas (pah-moan-hahs), which means little purses, are another favorite snack. They are a mixture of corn, coconut, sugar, and farofa that are wrapped in corn husks and folded to look like little packages. The tiny packets are steamed until the filling becomes soft and creamy.

Pamonhas are sold at special stands called pamon-harias (pah-moan-har-ee-ahs), as well as by traveling vendors. The traveling vendors sell the little treats from trucks that they drive around residential neighborhoods ringing bells and playing music to announce their presence. Upon hearing the trucks, hungry Brazilians hurry out to the street to get their favorite treats, which are sold wrapped in newspaper to keep them warm.

Brazilians love to top the sweet little pamonhas with hot pepper sauce. Mixing sweet and spicy flavors is very popular. Steamy hot, fresh, and delicious, these little treats are, according to chef Bateman, "the most common street food in São Paulo."[16] São Paulo is the largest city in Brazil.

Pamonhas, meaning "little purses," are popular sweet snacks that are often topped with hot pepper sauce.

Cheese Bread

Bread filled or coated with cheese is a popular salgahdino. This is an easy and tasty recipe. Many Brazilians top the toasted cheese bread with crushed cashew nuts. Because authentic cassava starch, from which Brazilian cheese bread is made, is hard to get in North America, this recipe has been adapted to use sliced bread.

Ingredients

6 slices of white bread, toasted and cut into halves
4 tablespoons soft cream cheese
4 tablespoons grated Parmesan cheese
1 tablespoon butter
2 eggs
½ teaspoon nutmeg

Instructions

1. Preheat the oven to 400 degrees.
2. Mix well all the ingredients, except the bread. Spread the mixture on the bread.
3. Spray a cookie sheet with nonstick spray. Put the bread on the cookie sheet. Bake until the cheese is melted.

Makes 12 little toasts.

Cheese bread is a delicious and popular snack.

Custards and Puddings

Custards and puddings are favorite sweet treats in Brazil. They are often served for dessert, or as a special snack. Flan, a caramel custard, is a popular favorite. Brazilian cooks learned to make it from Portuguese nuns who were skilled at making egg-based desserts. The Brazilian cooks gave the nuns' flan a tropical flavor by adding coconut to the recipe. Corn, oranges, tapioca, coffee, avocados, and prunes are other popular pudding flavors. Most are combined with coconut.

Flan with a tropical twist is a very popular dessert.

Along with fruits familiar to North Americans, many exotic varieties, such as sugar apples, are grown and sold in Brazil.

Thirst Quenching and Healthy

When Brazilians are thirsty, one of their favorite beverages is fruit juice. Brazilian juice bars are world famous. Here, people can choose from dozens of exotic tropical fruit juices, all freshly squeezed and loaded with vitamins and minerals. Customers choose whether they want their juice natural, or with sugar and water added, or with milk. The last is known as a vitamina (vee-tah-mee-nah) or vitamin special, because milk contains additional nutrients.

Banana Vitamina

Vitaminas are fruit juices made with milk. A cup of any type of fresh or frozen fruit can be used or combined. You can use whole, low-fat, nonfat, or soy milk.

Ingredients
1 banana, peeled, cut in four pieces, frozen
1 cup milk
1 tablespoon honey
2 tablespoons orange juice

Instructions
1. Put the ingredients in a blender and blend until it forms a smooth liquid.
2. Pour into glasses and add ice cubes to taste.

Serves 2.

Both children and adults love the taste of banana vitamina.

Some of the juices, like orange, grapefruit, or pineapple, are well-known in North America. Others are made from fruits that grow in the Amazon rain forest. **Acerola** (ah-ser-oh-la) is one such fruit. It looks like a cherry and has a delicious tart flavor. Besides being tasty, a glass of acerola juice contains ten times more vitamin C than an equal size glass of orange juice.

Acai (ah-sigh-ee) is another healthy tropical fruit. Similar to a blueberry in appearance and a raspberry in taste, it grows on palm trees that line the Amazon River. Acai is so loaded with vitamins and minerals that scientists call it a super food. In fact, in laboratory tests in which leukemia cells were bathed in acai juice, the cells died. As a result, researchers are doing more tests. Whether or not acai juice proves to be a cure for cancer

Coffee

Coffee beans are grown in Brazil, and coffee is a very popular drink. Brazilians drink the beverage all day long. Most businesses and government agencies serve coffee to their employees twice a day. Beauty salons, clothing shops, and jewelry stores greet their customers with coffee, too. It is always served at business meetings. And guests in Brazilian homes are welcomed with a steaming hot cup of the beverage. The coffee is very strong, which is why it is served in tiny cups. Brazilians rarely add milk or cream to their coffee. They prefer it black with lots of sugar.

Coffee is grown in Brazil and is so popular that many Brazilians drink several cups a day.

Fruit juice is a delicious way for Brazilians to get their vitamins.

remains to be seen. But one thing is certain: Brazilians love the delicious and healthy purple juice.

Other juices are also quite popular. There are juices made of watermelon, mangos, papayas, bananas, and carambolas or starfruits. Starfruit is a yellow fruit that looks like its namesake, a little star. There is also cupuacua, (coop-oo-ah-coo-ah) a sweet, long, yellow fruit and ata, or sugar apple. Sugar apple is a bumpy green fruit with a sweet white pulp that tastes similar to a pear. Bright yellow, purple, or red passion fruit is another favorite. The fruits are filled with dozens of tiny seeds and incredibly sweet pulp.

Cashew apple is another popular treat. It is shaped like a small yellow or red bell pepper with yellow pulp. Besides its delicious pearlike flavor, what is interesting about the cashew apple is that the apple itself is not really the fruit. The fruit is the cashew nut that grows from its tip.

Lime and coconut juices are favorites, too. Coconut juice is so popular that, in addition to being sold at juice bars, it is sold on streets and beaches by roaming vendors. A Brazilian travel article on the Web site Visaexpress.net explains, "coconut juice is available everywhere that it is hot and where there are people. With a few strokes of a butcher's knife, vendors open a hole large enough for a straw."[17]

Bright green limeade may be the most popular juice in Brazil. Lemons do not grow in Brazil. Instead, Brazilians grow limes that taste like a cross between lemons and limes. With the addition of water and sugar, they make a slightly sweet, slightly tart beverage that is an especially good thirst quencher on a hot day. And limes are loaded with vitamin C.

Sugarcane is also turned into juice. To do this, long sticks of sugarcane are pushed through the sides of a rectangular metal machine. A device in the machine crushes the cane and squeezes out the juice, which comes out of a spout on the front of the machine.

According to Visaexpress.com, no matter which kind of juice a Brazilian chooses, "all Brazilian juices are divine."[18] So too, are the many salgadihos that are sold everywhere. Their scent fills Brazilian streets, beaches, parks, and roadways. It is no wonder Brazilians love to snack. With so many choices, snacking is hard to resist.

chapter

4

Food for Festas

Brazilians love to get together with friends and family and have a **festa** (feh-stah), the Brazilian word for celebration. Almost any occasion is a chance to have fun. Whether it's a holiday or a special occasion, there are bound to be delicious foods that make the event more exciting.

A Family Gathering

Birthdays are a time to celebrate in Brazil. Children and adults, too, have birthday parties. And people of all ages attend. You'll find everyone from young children to great-grandparents mixing and mingling at a typical birthday festa. There are presents, hugs and kisses, and lots of fun and laughter. Salgadinhos like

A birthday is reason enough for a party.

empadinhas, fried shrimp, and little sandwiches sat-
isfy guests' hunger. But the main focus of the occasion
is the table of sweets. It is a large table offering a huge
selection.

The birthday cake is the centerpiece on the table of
sweets. Typically, it is a richly decorated theme cake
made special for the honoree. It might look like a soc-
cer field, or a fairytale castle. Or it may be shaped like
a heart to show how much the celebrant is loved. The
use of different colored icing and sugars makes Brazilian birthday cakes almost too beautiful to eat. But
their delicious taste makes them hard to resist. The
cakes may be bright gold from the many egg yolks used

The cake is the centerpiece of the birthday celebration.

A Rooftop Festa

Brazilians love celebrating so much that when a new building is finished, the owner of the building throws a party for the construction workers. What makes the party unusual is that it is held on the new building's roof. It does not matter how tall the building is. It can be a skyscraper or a one-story house. For the party, the roof is decorated with leafy branches. Sweets, sodas, and sandwiches are served.

Many people live in Brazil's largest cities, Rio de Janeiro and São Paulo.

to make them, or they may be deep dark chocolate. They may be filled with pineapple or oranges, or mixed with coconut or almonds.

The cake is surrounded by mountains of sweet treats or **doces** (dough-says), as they are called in Brazil. Each is wrapped in beautifully colored paper.

Some are placed in the petals of paper flowers that are strewn on the table, while others form glittering and vividly hued hills of sweets. "The table of sweets is wonderful to see," explains Dolores Botafogo. "A beautiful cake in a marvelous shape, intricately decorated, appropriate to the occasion; baskets, bowls, and plates of various sweets, beautifully wrapped in silver and gold paper or fringed tissue

Carnival in Brazil

For religious reasons, many Brazilians give up favorite foods in the period before Easter known as Lent. But before Lent begins, Brazilians throughout the country, and especially in Rio de Janiero, throw a giant street party known as Carnival. During this time, Brazilians wear elaborate costumes and hold parades with bands and dancing. There are contests for dancers who perform a Latin dance called the samba.

Although there are no specific Carnival foods, salgadinhos are sold everywhere. Banquet foods like turkey and ham are also popular. They are served at elegant balls held at private clubs in honor of Carnival.

Brazilians love parties, and the biggest one, called Carnival, is held every year throughout the country before Lent begins.

Mother-in-Law's Eyes

Use soft, pitted prunes for this recipe. The cloves are just for decoration. Do not eat them!

Ingredients
12 pitted prunes
1 cup grated coconut
1 egg yolk
⅓ cup sugar
⅓ cup water
12 cloves

Instructions
1. Put the sugar and water in a pot and cook over low heat, stirring until the sugar dissolves.
2. Add the egg yolk and coconut. Let the mix cook until it thickens, stirring often. Remove from the heat and let the mixture cool.
3. Hollow out the center of each prune. Put the coconut mixture into each hollow, spreading it carefully so that it looks like an eyeball. Put a clove in the center of each eyeball.
4. Serve in paper cupcake holders.

Makes 12

and cellophane; candies hidden in stems of soft-colored tissue flowers."[19]

Favorite Doces

Guests can choose from a wide variety of sweets. Many contain nuts or fruit, and every one is delicious. Some have names like angel's cheeks and coconut kisses,

Brigadeiros

These are not hard to make. You can use any type of chocolate powder in the recipe. Putting margarine on your hands makes it easier to form the chocolate balls.

Ingredients
12 ounce-can sweetened condensed milk
4 tablespoons chocolate powder
1 tablespoon margarine
1 cup chocolate sprinkles

Instructions
1. Heat the milk, margarine, and chocolate powder over low heat, stirring constantly. It's done when the mixture thickens and you can see the bottom of the pot.
2. Remove from heat. Pour the mixture on a greased plate and let it cool to room temperature.
3. When it is cool, roll it into 1–1 ½ inch balls. Top the balls with chocolate sprinkles. Put them in paper cupcake holders.

Makes 20.

Brigadeiros are named for a brigadier general in World War II.

that bring to mind their delicate flavors. Others, like mother-in-law's eyes, are named for the way they look. These sweets feature prunes stuffed with a coconut mixture and topped with a clove. The coconut mixture looks like an eyeball. And the clove in the center, which is removed before the treat is eaten, looks like a pupil. Though the idea of eating a sweet that looks like an eyeball may seem strange, the combination of prunes and coconut is deliciously sweet and chewy.

Brigadeiros (bree-gah-der-ee-ohs), or brigadiers, are another popular choice. They are chocolate fudge balls, named for Eduardo Gomes. He was a popular Brazilian air force brigadier general during World War II. No one can say for sure why the candies, made with cocoa powder, butter, and condensed milk, were named after the man. It may be because he was charming and brave—the type of man whom many women would have liked for a sweetheart.

Although Gomes is no longer alive, brigadeiros live on. "I love brigadeiros!" Lynn, who lives in Brazil, says, "chocolate, mmm, sweetened condensed milk, mmm, not exactly like fudge but similarly good-tasting!"[20]

Happily Married

Sweets also play an important role at Brazilian weddings. **Bem casados** (bem cah-sah-doughs), which means happily married, serve as a sweet wedding treat but also as a souvenir for wedding guests to take home when the party ends.

These delicacies are like little pastry sandwiches. They consist of two pieces of fluffy yellow cake cut into 2-inch (5.1cm) rings or hearts. These are filled with a kind of sweet cream called **doce de leite** (dough-say day leh-ee-teh) and rolled in powdered sugar.

Doce de leite starts out as thick syrup made from sugar, water, egg yolks, and condensed milk, which hardens into a sticky, sweet cream. It connects the two

Weddings, like this mass wedding ceremony in Rio de Janeiro, are a cause for celebration in Brazil.

pieces of cake just the way marriage connects a man and a woman. The pastry, according to an article on Wedding Guru, a Web site that looks at wedding traditions around the world, "is the most famous dessert in a wedding." It acts, the article explains, as "a symbol of unity."[21]

These pastries are so important that the families of prospective brides and grooms often go on tasting trips to dozens of bakeries in order to find the best bem casa-dos to serve at their wedding. The cakes must not only taste perfect, but they must look lovely too. Wrapped in tissue paper or cellophane to match the wedding colors and tied with pretty ribbons, the confections are displayed in a special area. Guests take one as a party favor as they leave. This is a way for the bride and groom to thank their guests for coming and for the guests to wish the couple a sweet life.

Christmas Celebrations

Christmas is another time for a festa. Brazilian families traditionally gather on Christmas Eve for a big supper, which is served anytime from 9 P.M. to well after midnight. Although the menu may vary, turkey is likely to be the main dish. The bird is native to South America, and Brazilians have been eating turkey for centuries. Probably because turkey takes a long time to cook, Brazilians have come to associate it with special occasions like Christmas.

Brazilians prepare turkey differently than most North Americans do. First, they marinate the bird in

Turkey is native to South America and is often served for Christmas Eve supper.

a mixture made with lime, onions, tomato, garlic, and an alcoholic beverage called cachaca (cah-chah-cah). Since the alcohol acts as a preservative, this practice was very important in the past, especially because Brazil is in the Southern Hemisphere and Christmas falls in the hottest part of the year. Without refrigeration, turkey spoils easily.

Modern Brazilians have refrigerators and do not have to worry about the turkey spoiling. But, because they like the tangy flavor the marinade adds, they have continued to use it. And because the alcohol burns off during cooking, no one has to worry about its effects.

The turkey usually marinates overnight. Before it is placed in the oven, it is stuffed. The stuffing, too, is distinctively Brazilian. For those who like a salty smoky taste, the stuffing can be made of pork, ham, bacon, hard-boiled eggs, onions, and farofa. Or, for those who prefer sweeter stuffing, dried fruit is substituted for the meat.

Once the turkey is in the oven, many Brazilian cooks baste it with another uniquely Brazilian ingredient, coffee with cream and sugar. It gives the turkey a lovely brown color, an enchanting aroma, and produces bittersweet gravy.

Rice and kale, a leafy green vegetable that is quite popular, usually accompanies the turkey. The kale is sautéed in garlic and oil for only a few minutes. That way it remains crisp and tasty.

The meal is filling and delicious. Irene, who grew up in Brazil, recalls: "A typical Christmas dinner includes turkey . . . rice, nuts, and fresh vegetables, and fruit dishes. Our family gatherings at Christmas and the family dinner are joyful memories of my past."[22]

Many Brazilians' fondest memories include turkey at Christmas, the table of sweets at birthday parties, and bem casados at weddings. These foods are a big part of Brazilian festas and make these events more memorable and more fun.

Metric Conversions

Mass (weight)

1 ounce (oz.)	= 28.0 grams (g)
8 ounces	= 227.0 grams
1 pound (lb.) or 16 ounces	= 0.45 kilograms (kg)
2.2 pounds	= 1.0 kilogram

Liquid Volume

1 teaspoon (tsp.)	= 5.0 milliliters (ml)
1 tablespoon (tbsp.)	= 15.0 milliliters
1 fluid ounce (oz.)	= 30.0 milliliters
1 cup (c.)	= 240 milliliters
1 pint (pt.)	= 480 milliliters
1 quart (qt.)	= 0.96 liters (l)
1 gallon (gal.)	= 3.84 liters

Pan Sizes

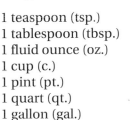

8- inch cake pan	= 20 x 4-centimeter cake pan
9-inch cake pan	= 23 x 3.5-centimeter cake pan
11 x 7-inch baking pan	= 28 x 18-centimeter baking pan
13 x 9-inch baking pan	= 32.5 x 23-centimeter baking pan
9 x 5-inch loaf pan	= 23 x 13-centimeter loaf pan
2-quart casserole	= 2-liter casserole

Temperature

212°F	= 100°C (boiling point of water)
225°F	= 110°C
250°F	= 120°C
275°F	= 135°C
300°F	= 150°C
325°F	= 160°C
350°F	= 180°C
375°F	= 190°C
400°F	= 200°C

Length

1/4 inch (in.)	= 0.6 centimeters (cm)
1/2 inch	= 1.25 centimeters
1 inch	= 2.5 centimeters

Notes

Chapter 1: Food Rooted in the Past

1. Christopher Idone, *Brazil: A Cook's Tour*. New York: Random House, 1995, p. xiii.

2. "Mandioca Frita," Maria-Brazil, www.maria-brazil.org/mandioca_frita.htm.

3. Quoted in Norman Van Aken, *New World Kitchen*. New York: HarperCollins, 2003, p. 188.

4. Michael Bateman, *Café Brazil*. Lincolnwood, IL: Contemporary Books, 1999, p. 44.

5. Dolores Botafogo, *The Art of Brazilian Cookery*. New York: Hippocrene Books, 1960, p. 129.

6. Botafogo, *The Art of Brazilian Cookery*. p. 129.

Chapter 2: Different Regions, Different Dishes

7. "Brazil National Dish: Feijoada Recipe and Restaurants," Brazilmax.com, www.brazilmax.com/news.cfm/tborigem/fe_fooddrink/id/11.

8. Joan B. Peterson, *Eat Smart in Brazil*. Madison, WI: Ginkgo Press, 2006, p. 31.

9. Van Aken, *New World Kitchen*. p. 188.

10. Botafogo, *The Art of Brazilian Cookery*. p. 126.

11. Manny Howard, "A Four Star Chef in a Movie Star's Brazil," *Food and Wine*, February 2006, p. 109.

12. Rosa, "Moqueca de Peixe," Rosa's Yummy Yums, November 28, 2005, www.rosas-yummy-yums.blogspot.com/2005/11/moqueca-de-peixe.html.

Chapter 3: Tasty Snacks and Healthy Drinks

13. "Empadas," Maria-Brazil, www.maria-brazil.org/empadas.htm.

14. Idone, *Brazil: A Cook's Tour.* p. 97.

15. "Food and Eating Out in Salvador, Bahia," Bahia-Online, www.bahia-online.net/FoodinSalvador.htm.

16. Bateman, *Café Brazil.* p. 22.

17. "Food and Drink," Visaexpress.net, www.visaexpress.net/brazil/food_drink.htm.

18. "Food and Drink," Visaexpress.net.

Chapter 4: Food for Festas

19. Botafogo, *The Art of Brazilian Cookery.* p. 23.

20. Lynn de Oliveira, Interview with the author, January 28, 2007.

21. "Brazilian Weddings," Wedding Guru, www.weddingguru.com/wt_articles.asp?pk=21&group=3.

22. "Christmas Memories," Irene's Country Corner, www.irenescorner.com/homc/christmas/memories/index.htm.

Glossary

acai: A nutritious berrylike fruit.

acarajes: Bean and shrimp fritters.

acerola: A cherrylike fruit.

bem casados: A pastry served at weddings.

brigadeiros: Fudge balls.

churrasco: Brazilian barbecue.

dende oil: Cooking oil made from the nuts of a palm tree.

doce de leite: Sweet cream.

doces: Sweets.

empadinhas: Little snack pies.

farinha de mandioca: Flour made from cassava.

farofa: Toasted cassava flour.

feijoada: A bean-and-pork stew, which is the national dish of Brazil.

festa: A party or celebration.

gauchos: Brazilian cowboys.

manioc: A starchy root vegetable also known as cassava, mandioca, or yuca.

moqueca: Seafood stew.

pamonhas: Corn husks filled with a corn and coconut mixture.

pampas: Brazilian plains.

pastel: An empadinha that is fried rather than baked.

refogado: A method of cooking in which ingredients such as meat, fish, or rice are lightly fried with garlic, onions, and tomatoes.

salgadihos: Salty snacks.

For Further Exploration

Books

Alison Behnke, *Cooking the Brazilian Way*. Minneapolis: Lerner, 2004. A Brazilian recipe book for children.

Malika Hollander, *Brazil: The Culture*. New York: Crabtree, 2003. Brazilian culture, food, and holidays are discussed.

Mathhew Locricchio, *The Cooking of Brazil*. New York: Benchmark Books, 2004. A Brazilian recipe book for children.

Mariana Serra, *Brazil*. Austin, TX: Raintree Steck-Vaughn, 2000. A look at Brazilian festivals and the foods associated with them.

Web Sites

Brazilian Embassy "Kid's Corner," (www.brasilemb.org/kids_corner/kids1.shtml). Pictures, games, and information about Brazil, including pictures of Amazon rain forest animals and facts about Brazilian sea turtles.

Cook Brazil (www.cookbrazil.com/index.htm). A Brazilian cooking Web site with dozens of recipes.

Fact Monster "Brazil" (www.factmonster.com/ce6/world/A0808783.html). Information on Brazilian history, geography, culture, economics, and daily life written for kids.

Maria-Brazil (www.maria-brazil.org). A Web site geared to adults, but interesting for kids, dedicated to Brazilian culture. There are pictures of Brazil, many recipes, and music and folklore.

Index

Picture Credits

About the Author

Barbara Sheen is the author of numerous works of fiction and nonfiction for young people, including more than a dozen books in the Taste of Culture series. She lives in New Mexico with her family. In her spare time, she likes to swim, walk, garden, and read. Of course, she loves to cook!